BE YOUR BEST

EMPATHY

Shannon Welbourn

AV2
www.av2books.com

AV2

Step 1
Go to **www.av2books.com**

Step 2
Enter this unique code
FQMXKF607

Step 3
Explore your interactive eBook!

AV2 is optimized for use on any device

Your interactive eBook comes with...

Contents
Browse a live contents page to easily navigate through resources

Audio
Listen to sections of the book read aloud

Videos
Watch informative video clips

Weblinks
Gain additional information for research

Try This!
Complete activities and hands-on experiments

Key Words
Study vocabulary, and complete a matching word activity

Quizzes
Test your knowledge

Slideshows
View images and captions

... and much, much more!

View new titles and product videos at **www.av2books.com**

BE YOUR BEST

EMPATHY

Contents

What Is Empathy?

Have you ever heard the saying, "Try to put yourself in someone else's shoes"? This means that you should try to understand another person's point of view.

Looking at things from another person's viewpoint helps you develop empathy. Empathy means thinking about what other people are thinking and feeling. When you **express** empathy, you have **compassion** for others. You show concern for their feelings.

Empathy helps you understand others' feelings under different circumstances.

We all have the ability to express empathy toward others. Empathy is a skill you can develop. You can show and develop empathy by taking time to listen to others express their feelings, and by being **respectful** of what they say. As you build your empathy, you become more aware of the people around you.

Show your empathy by listening to what others have to say.

Why Is Empathy Important?

Empathy is an important skill to develop. Learning to understand how someone else is feeling can help you build relationships.

People who have empathy **value** the thoughts and feelings of others. To value something means to recognize that it is important. They show this by trying hard to understand why someone feels or acts in a certain way. People with empathy try to understand others' feelings before they react or respond to them. This helps them respond in a more thoughtful way.

Showing empathy can help you build strong friendships throughout your life.

When people use empathy to understand others' feelings, they build strong relationships. When you listen to someone's feelings, you show them that you can be trusted. Empathy can also help people avoid **conflict**, such as an argument. This is because people with empathy try to understand what makes others feel the way they do first, instead of reacting with anger. Approaching a problem with empathy can help you deal with it fairly.

BIOGRAPHY

Jayda Smith-Atkins

When Jayda Smith-Atkins felt the cold winter approaching, she knew that the people without homes in her community would need help.

On her eighth birthday, Jayda decided to show empathy for people without homes in her community. Jayda felt the cold weather outside and imagined what it would be like to spend the winter without coats, mittens, scarves, and hats to keep warm. She put herself in the shoes of those without homes or warm clothing, and knew that they needed help. With the help of her mother, Jayda collected old winter clothing from friends, family, and other members of her community.

NAME: **Jayda Smith-Atkins**
FROM: **Halifax, Nova Scotia, Canada**
ACCOMPLISHMENT:
Helped give warm clothes to people without homes in her community

Each piece of warm clothing had a tag attached so people knew they could use it to keep warm.

She and seven of her friends set out on her birthday to leave the clothing around their community, so that people who needed warmth could find the clothing easily. She and her friends put the needs of others before their own. They showed amazing empathy by making warm clothing as accessible and useful as possible for others in their community. People around the world are also using this idea now and showing their empathy for others in their communities.

January is Halifax's coldest month. The average low temperature is about **17°** Fahrenheit. (-8° Celsius)

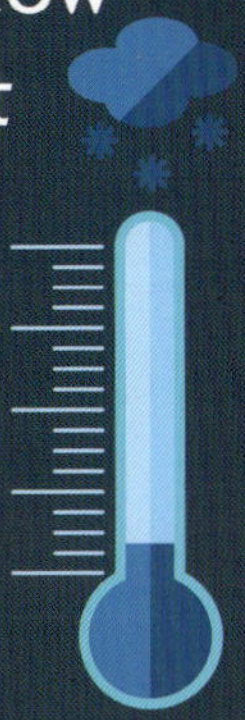

There are more than **560,000** homeless people in the United States.

New York City is the city with the largest homeless population in the United States. More than **92,000** homeless people live there.

Empathy at Home

Expressing empathy at home can help you build strong relationships with each member of your family.

It is important for family members to feel that they are supported by each other. Try to show your support for your family by understanding their feelings. When all members of a family express empathy, they avoid conflict at home.

You may hear one of your family members talking about the bad day they had. You can express your empathy by offering to listen to them talk about their feelings. You can try to understand why they are upset. Maybe your little sister is upset because she lost her favorite toy. You might not understand why she is so upset, but you can show empathy by listening to her feelings before reacting to her **situation**. Once she explains how she feels, you can express your empathy by telling her about a time you felt the same way.

Show your empathy at home by listening to your family members' feelings before you respond or react to problems.

Empathy at School

Showing empathy at school helps others see that you can be a good friend.

Show your classmates you care. Be understanding of them. Respect others' differences and think about how you are the same. Finding what you have in common can help you develop empathy.

Learn to Make Decisions

What is one way that you can show a classmate that you respect their feelings?

We can show empathy at school by seeing things from our classmates' points of view.

Think of a time that someone put his or her hand up in class to answer a question. What happened if he or she gave an incorrect answer? How did others respond? Maybe someone laughed or made a joke about the incorrect answer. Those responses would be hurtful and do not show empathy. We can all relate to how it feels to raise your hand in class or be called upon to answer. Sometimes, it can be scary. Think about how you would feel if others laughed at your answer. Understanding how your classmate may feel in this type of situation helps you show empathy.

Empathy in Your Community

A community is a group of people who live, work, and play in a place. Your home, school, and neighborhood are part of your community.

Part of developing empathy is having **open-mindedness**. To be open-minded is to look at things from many different points of view and be accepting of many ways to think or do things. There are many different people in your community. You may not always know them.

One way to show your empathy in your community is to help others. You could collect food or clothing to give to those who need it.

When you are open-minded toward all of the people in your community, it means that you try to see their **perspective** before making your own **assumptions** about them. You can develop your open-mindedness by learning about many different types of people. Maybe you can join a new club or sit with a new group of students at lunch. Showing empathy in your community means that you take time to learn about people's situations, perspectives, and feelings.

CASE STUDY

Buddy Benches

Buddy Benches are tools that help children learn empathy. The benches encourage children to depend on each other, develop friendships, and listen to each other's feelings.

When children are playing outside at recess, they could feel left out. Some children may feel lonely. Others may feel they do not belong. Buddy benches are places where children can sit when they need someone to talk to. Sitting on the bench is a way that children can show that they need help without saying it. When other children see someone sitting on the bench, they can talk to the person on the bench or invite them to play.

Buddy Benches can be found on playgrounds around the world. Children everywhere use them to feel included and develop empathy.

An important part of empathy is being able to understand other people's feelings, even if they do not say them out loud. Buddy Benches help kids develop this part of empathy because they recognize how a person might be feeling when they sit on the bench. Buddy Benches encourage children to express their empathy for each other by respectfully listening to others' feelings and relating to them.

The idea for **Buddy Benches** first came to Christian Buck, a Pennsylvania elementary school student, in 2013.

Christian was only in **first grade** when he had the idea for Buddy Benches.

About **2,000** schools in the United States have buddy benches.

Overcoming Challenges

You will develop your empathy over time as you learn to accept others and appreciate differences.

Showing empathy toward others is not something you do once and check off a list. It becomes a part of who you are as a person.

The tips listed below can help you develop your empathy.

- If you do not understand how someone is feeling, ask questions to help. Listen to their answers.
- Remember that listening is more than just hearing what others say—it is understanding what you hear.
- Relate to others by remembering a time that you felt the same way. Share your experiences with them.
- You can express empathy with your words and actions. You might say words of encouragement to someone or do something nice for them.

Learn to Make Decisions

Think of a time someone showed you empathy. What words and actions did they use to express their feelings?

Encouraging Empathy in Others

One of the best ways you can encourage empathy in others is by being a good example yourself.

When you express empathy toward others, you are a **role model** for them to follow. Your example can encourage them to develop their empathy skills, too. Everyone can develop empathy.

Think back to the example of someone in class giving the wrong answer. If a classmate laughed, you can remind the classmate to think about how he or she would feel in the same situation. It is important not to make assumptions before learning a person's point of view. Encourage people to look at situations from the other person's perspective. What might the other person's thoughts and feelings be? Encourage kindness and understanding in every situation. Express your empathy!

Learn to Make Decisions

What would you do if you saw someone who was not being respectful or thoughtful toward someone else?

Empathy in Action

We show empathy by using words and actions that make people feel important, respected, and valued. We can grow and develop empathy with effort and practice.

Read each situation described below and answer the following questions. Then, share your ideas with a friend.

- How do you think the people in each situation feel?
- What could you say and do to show empathy?

Your brother studied very hard for a history test. When he gets the test back, his mark is much lower than he thought it would be.

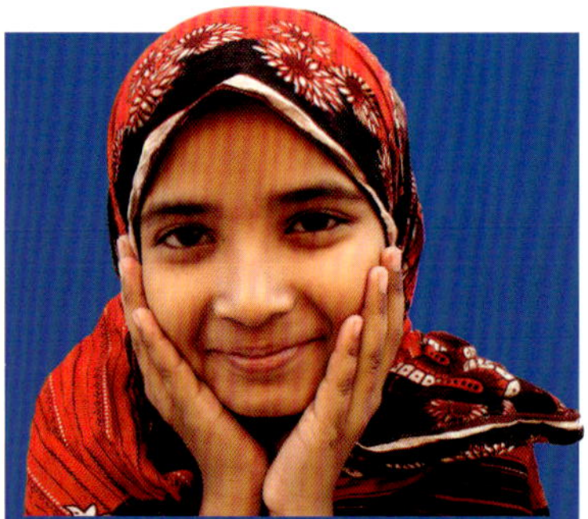

A new student joins your class in the middle of the year. She is from a different country and knows only a few words in English. Other kids make fun of the way she speaks.

Your soccer team wins the championship game in overtime. As you and your teammates cheer and celebrate, you see players from the other team standing quietly nearby.

Key Words

assumptions: things supposed to be true without evidence; taken for granted
circumstances: conditions or details of a situation, time, or place
community: a group of people who live, work, and play in a place
compassion: feeling concern for another
conflict: a clash or incompatible difference of ideas, interests, or goals
express: to show or put into words and actions
open-mindedness: to be accepting of different ideas and perspectives
perspective: a person's view or way of thinking about something
respectful: describing someone who is polite and gives appropriate attention to others
role model: a person who is respected by others
situation: circumstances or position at a given moment
value: to place importance on something

Index

Get the best of both worlds.

AV2 bridges the gap between print and digital.

The expandable resources toolbar enables quick access to content including **videos**, **audio**, **activities**, **weblinks**, **slideshows**, **quizzes**, and **key words**.

Animated videos make static images come alive.

Resource icons on each page help readers to further **explore key concepts**.

Published by AV2
350 5th Avenue, 59th Floor
New York, NY 10118
Website: www.av2books.com

Library of Congress Control Number: 2020937066

ISBN 978-1-7911-3158-6 (Hardcover)
ISBN 978-1-7911-3159-3 (Softcover)
ISBN 978-1-7911-3160-9 (Multi-user eBook)
ISBN 978-1-7911-3161-6 (Single-user eBook)

Printed in Guangzhou, China
1 2 3 4 5 6 7 8 9 0 24 23 22 21 20

042020
101119

Project Coordinator: Sara Cucini Designer: Jean Faye Marie Rodriguez

The publisher acknowledges Getty Images, iStock and Shutterstock as its primary image suppliers for this title.

First published by Crabtree Publishing Company in 2017.